FIFTY-SEVEN SONGS

FOR VOICE AND PIANO

RICHARD STRAUSS

DOVER PUBLICATIONS, INC.
NEW YORK

BIBLIOGRAPHICAL NOTE

This Dover edition, first published in 1993, is a republication of individual songs originally published by various publishers, as follows: Jos. Aibl, Munich (Op.10, Op.19, Op.21, Op.26, Op.27, Op.29, Op.32, Op.36, Op.37), O. B. Boise, London (Op.22), Ed. Bote and G. Bock, Berlin (Op.56), C. A. Challier, Berlin (Op.43), Rob. Forberg, Leipzig (Op.39), Adolph Fürstner, Berlin (Op.46, Op.47, Op.48, Op.49), F. E. C. Leuckart, Leipzig (Op.41) and Daniel Rahter, Hamburg (Op.15, Op.17). The German texts have been translated into English by Stanley Appelbaum specially for this edition. A list of sources of the texts, an alphabetical list of first lines and a glossary of German words and phrases have been newly added.

INTERNATIONAL STANDARD BOOK NUMBER: 0-486-27828-X

Manufactured in the United States of America
Dover Publications, Inc., 31 East 2nd Street, Mineola, N.Y. 11501

CONTENTS

Dates are those of composition.

ALPHABETICAL LIST OF FIRST LINES	v
SOURCES OF THE TEXTS	vi
GLOSSARY OF GERMAN WORDS AND PHRASES	vii

FROM OP. 10, ACHT GEDICHTE AUS "LETZTE BLÄTTER" VON HERMANN GILM (1885)

No. 1	Zueignung	1
No. 2	Nichts	3
No. 3	Die Nacht	5
No. 8	Allerseelen	7

FROM OP. 15, FÜNF LIEDER (1884–1886)

No. 1	Madrigal	10
No. 2	Winternacht	13
No. 5	Heimkehr	17

FROM OP. 17, SECHS LIEDER VON A. F. VON SCHACK (1885–1887)

No. 2	Ständchen	19
No. 5	Nur Mut!	25
No. 6	Barkarole	29

FROM OP. 19, SECHS LIEDER AUS "LOTOSBLÄTTER" VON A. F. VON SCHACK (1885–1888)

No. 6	"Mein Herz ist stumm"	33

FROM OP. 21, SCHLICHTE WEISEN. FÜNF GEDICHTE VON FELIX DAHN (1887–1888)

No. 1	"All mein Gedanken"	36
No. 2	"Du meines Herzens Krönelein"	38
No. 3	"Ach Lieb, ich muss nun scheiden!"	40
No. 4	"Ach weh mir unglückhaftem Mann"	42
No. 5	"Die Frauen sind oft fromm und still"	46

FROM OP. 22, MÄDCHENBLUMEN. GEDICHTE VON FELIX DAHN (1886–1888)

No. 1	Kornblumen	48
No. 2	Mohnblumen	51
No. 3	Epheu	54
No. 4	Wasserrose	58

FROM OP. 26, ZWEI LIEDER (NACH NIKOLAUS LENAU) (1891)

No. 1	Frühlingsgedränge	65

FROM OP. 27, VIER LIEDER (1894)

No. 1	Ruhe, meine Seele!	69
No. 3	Heimliche Aufforderung	71
No. 4	Morgen!	77

FROM OP. 29, DREI LIEDER NACH GEDICHTEN VON OTTO JULIUS BIERBAUM (1895)

No. 1	Traum durch die Dämmerung	79

FROM OP. 32, FÜNF LIEDER (1896)

No. 1	"Ich trage meine Minne"	82
No. 2	Sehnsucht	85
No. 3	Liebeshymnus	89
No. 4	O süsser Mai!	91
No. 5	Himmelsboten	95

FROM OP. 36, VIER LIEDER (1897–1898)

No. 1	Das Rosenband	99
No. 2	Für funfzehn Pfennige	102
No. 3	Hat gesagt—bleibt's nicht dabei	107

FROM OP. 37, SECHS LIEDER (1896–1898)

No. 2	Ich liebe dich	111
No. 4	Mein Auge	115
No. 5	Herr Lenz	118

FROM OP. 39, FÜNF LIEDER (1898)

No. 2	Junghexenlied	121
No. 3	Der Arbeitsmann	126
No. 5	Lied an meinen Sohn	131

iv

FROM OP. 41, FÜNF LIEDER (1899)

No. 2   In der Campagna   140
No. 3   Am Ufer   145
No. 4   Bruder Liederlich   148

FROM OP. 43, DREI GESÄNGE ÄLTERER
DEUTSCHER DICHTER (1899)

No. 1   An Sie   156

FROM OP. 46, FÜNF GEDICHTE VON FRIEDRICH
RÜCKERT (1899–1900)

No. 2   "Gestern war ich Atlas"   163
No. 3   Die sieben Siegel   167
No. 5   Ich sehe wie in einem Spiegel   172

FROM OP. 47, FÜNF LIEDER (LUDWIG UHLAND)
(1900)

No. 5   Von den sieben Zechbrüdern   178

FROM OP. 48, FÜNF LIEDER NACH GEDICHTEN
VOM OTTO JULIUS BIERBAUM UND KARL
HENCKELL (1900)

No. 1   Freundliche Vision   198
No. 3   Kling! . . .   201
No. 4   Winterweihe   205

FROM OP. 49, ACHT LIEDER (1901)

No. 2   In goldener Fülle   208
No. 4   Das Lied des Steinklopfers   214

FROM OP. 56, SECHS LIEDER (1903–1906)

No. 1   Gefunden   220
No. 2   Blindenklage   223
No. 3   Im Spätboot   228
No. 5   Frühlingsfeier   232
No. 6   Die heiligen drei Könige aus
Morgenland   240

TRANSLATIONS OF THE TEXTS   245

ALPHABETICAL LIST OF FIRST LINES

Aber Epheu nenn' ich jene Mädchen	54
Ach Lieb, ich muss nun scheiden!	40
Ach weh mir unglückhaftem Mann	42
All mein Gedanken, mein Herz und mein Sinn	36
Als Nachts ich überm Gebirge ritt	121
Auf, hebe die funkelnde Schale empor zum Mund	71
Aus dem Walde tritt die Nacht	5
Aus der Schiffsbank mach' ich meinen Pfühl	228
Das ist des Frühlings traurige Lust!	232
Das Mägdlein will ein' Freier hab'n	102
Der Mondschein, der ist schon verblichen	95
Der Sturm behorcht mein Vaterhaus	131
Die Feder am Sturmhut in Spiel und Gefahren	148
Die Frauen sind oft fromm und still	46
Die heil'gen drei Kön'ge aus Morgenland	240
Die Welt verstummt, dein Blut erklingt	145
Du bist mein Auge! Du durchdringst mich ganz	115
Du meines Herzens Krönelein	38
Frühlingskinder im bunten Gedränge	65
Gestern war ich Atlas, der den Himmel trug	163
Heil jenem Tag, der dich geboren	89
Herr Lenz springt heute durch die Stadt	118
Ich bin kein Minister	214
Ich ging den Weg entlang, der einsam lag	85
Ich ging im Walde	220
Ich grüsse die Sonne, die dort versinkt	140
Ich kenne sieben lust'ge Brüder	178
Ich sehe wie in einem Spiegel	172
Ich trage meine Minne vor Wonne	82
Im Frühlingsschatten fand ich sie	99
In diesen Wintertagen	205
In's Joch beug' ich den Nacken demutvoll	10
Ja, du weisst es teure Seele	1
Kennst du die Blume, die märchenhafte	58
Kling! . . .	201
Kornblumen nenn' ich die Gestalten	48
Lass' das Zagen, trage mutig	25
Leiser schwanken die Äste	17
Mach' auf, mach' auf, doch leise mein Kind	19
Mein Herz ist stumm, mein Herz ist kalt	33
Mein Vater hat gesagt, ich soll das Kindlein wiegen	107
Mit Regen und Sturmgebrause	13
Mohnblumen sind die runden	51
Nennen soll ich, sagt ihr, meine	3
Nicht ein Lüftchen regt sich leise	69
Nicht im Schlafe hab ich das geträumt	198
O süsser Mai, o habe du Erbarmen	91
Stell' auf den Tisch die duftenden Reseden	7
Um der fallenden Ruder Spitzen	29
Und morgen wird die Sonne wieder scheinen	77
Vier adlige Rosse	111
Weil ich dich nicht legen kann	167
Weite Wiesen im Dämmergrau	79
Wenn ich dich frage, dem das Leben blüht	223
Wir haben ein Bett, wir haben ein Kind	126
Wir schreiten in goldener Fülle	208
Zeit, Verkündigerin der besten Freuden	156

SOURCES OF THE TEXTS

OTTO JULIUS BIERBAUM (1865–1910)
Traum durch die Dämmerung Op.29 No.1
Junghexenlied Op.39 No.2
Freundliche Vision Op.48 No.1

EMANUEL VON BODMAN (1874–1946)
Herr Lenz Op.37 No.5

MICHELANGELO BUONARROTI (1475–1564; German translation by Sophie Hasenclever)
Madrigal Op.15 No.1

(JULIUS SOPHUS) FELIX DAHN (1834–1912)
"All mein Gedanken" Op.21 No.1
"Du meines Herzens Krönelein" Op.21 No.2
"Ach Lieb, ich muss nun scheiden!" Op.21 No.3
"Ach weh mir unglückhaftem Mann" Op.21 No.4
"Die Frauen sind oft fromm und still" Op.21 No.5
Mädchenblumen:
Kornblumen Op.22 No.1
Mohnblumen Op.22 No.2
Epheu Op.22 No.3
Wasserrose Op.22 No.4

RICHARD DEHMEL (1863–1920)
Mein Auge Op.37 No.4
Der Arbeitsmann Op.39 No.3
Lied an meinen Sohn Op.39 No.5
Am Ufer Op.41 No.3

HERMANN VON GILM [ZU ROSENEGG] (1812–1864)
Zueignung Op.10 No.1
Nichts Op.10 No.2
Die Nacht Op.10 No.3
Allerseelen Op.10 No.8

JOHANN WOLFGANG VON GOETHE (1749–1832)
Gefunden Op.56 No.1

HEINRICH HEINE (1797–1856)
Frühlingsfeier Op.56 No.5
Die heiligen drei Könige aus Morgenland Op. 56 No.6

KARL HENCKELL (1864–1929)
Ruhe, meine Seele! Op.27 No.1
"Ich trage meine Minne" Op.32 No.1

Liebeshymnus Op.32 No.3
O süsser Mai! Op.32 No.4
Kling! . . . Op.48 No.3
Winterweihe Op.48 No.4
Das Lied des Steinklopfers Op.49 No.4
Blindenklage Op.56 No.2

FRIEDRICH GOTTLIEB KLOPSTOCK (1724–1803)
Das Rosenband Op.36 No.1
An Sie Op.43 No.1

NIKOLAUS LENAU [PSEUDONYM OF NIKOLAUS NIEMBSCH VON STREHLENAU] (1802–1850)
Frühlingsgedränge Op.26 No.1

DETLEV VON LILIENCRON (1844–1909)
Sehnsucht Op.32 No.2
Ich liebe dich Op.37 No.2
Bruder Liederlich Op.41 No.4

JOHN HENRY MACKAY (1864–1933)
Heimliche Aufforderung Op.27 No.3
Morgen! Op.27 No.4
In der Campagna Op.41 No.2

CONRAD FERDINAND MEYER (1825–1898)
Im Spätboot Op.56 No.3

PAUL REMER (B. 1867)
In goldener Fülle Op.49 No.2

FRIEDRICH RÜCKERT (1788–1866)
"Gestern war ich Atlas" Op.46 No.2
Die sieben Siegel Op.46 No.3
Ich sehe wie in einem Spiegel Op.46 No.5

ADOLF FRIEDRICH VON SCHACK (1815–1894)
Winternacht Op.15 No.2
Heimkehr Op.15 No.5
Ständchen Op.17 No.2
Nur Mut! Op.17 No.5
Barkarole Op.17 No.6
"Mein Herz ist stumm" Op.19 No.6

LUDWIG UHLAND (1787–1862)
Von den sieben Zechbrüdern Op.47 No.5

FROM *DES KNABEN WUNDERHORN*
Himmelsboten Op.32 No.5
Für funfzehn Pfennige Op.36 No.2
Hat gesagt—bleibt's nicht dabei Op.36 No.3

GLOSSARY OF GERMAN WORDS AND PHRASES

aber, but
allmählich, gradually
(allmählich) immer mehr beschleunigen, (gradually) still more *accelerando*
allmählich wieder früheres Zeitmass, gradually returning to the earlier tempo
aufleuchtend, shining out
ausdrucksvoll, expressive
äusserst, extremely, utmost

begeistert, inspired
belebend, enlivened
bewegt(er), (more) animated
breit, broad

drängend, hurrying, stringendo
dreitaktig, three-measure phrase
dumpf, dully

ebenso rasch, just as rapidly
einfach, simple
enthusiastisch, enthusiastically
etwas, somewhat
etwas steigern, auch im Zeitmass, intensify somewhat, in tempo as well

feierlich, solemnly
feurig, fiery
Frau, Mrs.
frei im Vortrag, freely in execution
freundschaftlich(st), (most) amicably

geb[oren], née
gebunden, legato, metrical
gefühlvoll, tenderly
gemütlich, good-natured
Gesang, voice
getragen, sostenuto, solemn
gewidmet, dedicated
gleichsam vor sich hinsummend, as if crooning to himself
gleichsam wie mit einer Verbeugung, as if with a bow
grossherzogl[icher] Kammersänger, singer to the Archduke

heftig, violent

heiter, bright, serene
Herr(n), (to) Mister

im ersten Zeitmass, in the original tempo (Tempo I)
im übermütigen Frühlingston, in the high-spirited sound of Spring
im Zeitmass, in tempo
immer, always, still
immer ruhiger werden, becoming calmer and calmer
innig, heartfelt

jauchzend, exultant

k[öniglicher] b[ayerischer] Kammersänger, singer to the King of Bavaria
kurz, short
kurz gestossen, staccato in brief spurts

langsam(er), slow(er)
lebhaft, lively
leicht, light
leichthin, casually
Leidenschaftlich bewegt, with impassioned movement
lieb, dear
lustig, gay

mässig, moderately
meinen lieben Schwiegereltern, to my dear parents-in-law
mit, with
mit grösster Verachtung, with the greatest contempt
mit Laune, capriciously
Mutter, mother

nicht, not, do not

pfiffig, sly, cunning

ruhig(er), calm(er)

schleppen, drag
schmachtend, yearning
schnell(er), quick(er)
schnippisch, impertinent
schwungvoll, enthusiastic

sehr, very
sinnend, pensive, meditative
so schnell als möglich, as fast as possible
steigern(d), intensify(ing)
Steigerung, increasing intensity
stets, always, constantly, steadily
stolz, arrogant, haughty

treu, faithfully

und, and

verehrungsvoll, respectfully
verklingend, fading away
viertaktig, four-measure phrase

von hier ab nur mehr mit halber Stimme, from here on
  only *a mezza voce*

wählerisch, fussy
warm, warmly
Weihe, dedication, consecration
wieder, again
wie verzweifelt, as if in despair

zart, sweet
zärtlich, affectionate
zögernd, hesitant
zu, too
zugeeignet, dedicated to
zweitaktig, two-measure phrase .

FIFTY-SEVEN SONGS

FOR VOICE AND PIANO

Zueignung

Op. 10 №1

Ja, du weisst es teu - - re See - le, dass ich fern von dir___ mich quä - le,

Lie - be macht die Her - zen krank, ha - be Dank.

Einst hielt ich, der Frei - heit Ze - cher, hoch den A - me -

1

2

Nichts

Op. 10 Nº 2

Nen - nen soll ich, sagt ihr, mei - ne Kö - ni - gin im

Lie - der - reich? To - ren, die ihr seid, ich ken - ne sie am we - nig - sten von euch.

Fragt mich nach der Au - gen Far - be,

Die Nacht

Op. 10 Nº 3

Al - les nimmt sie, was nur hold, nimmt das Sil - ber weg des Stroms,

nimmt vom Kup-fer-dach des Doms weg das Gold.

Aus-ge-plün - dert steht der Strauch, rük-ke nä - her, Seel' an See -

le; o die Nacht, mir bangt, sie steh - le

dich mir auch.

Allerseelen

Op. 10 N⁰ 8

Gib mir die Hand, daß ich sie heim-lich drük - ke, und wenn man's sieht, _____ mir ist es ei - ner-lei, gib mir nur ei - nen dei - ner sü - ßen Blik - ke, wie einst im Mai. Es blüht und duf - tet heut' auf je - dem

Madrigal

Op. 15 N⁰ 1

Winternacht

Op. 15 No. 2

-lieb - te Her - rin wohnt.

molto cresc.

ff

Nie hab' ich die

Blü - te des Mai - - en, den blau - en - den

Him - mel, den bli - tzen - den Tau so fröh - lich ge - grüßt,

wie heu - te dein Schneien, dein Ne-bel-ge-bräu und Wol -

- ken - grau; denn durch das Flok - ken - ge -

- trie - be, schö - ner, als je - der Lenz ge -

- lacht, leuch-tet und blüht der Früh - ling der Lie - be mir

16

Heimkehr

Op. 15 № 5

Ständchen

Op. 17 № 2

Drum lei - se mein Mädchen, dass nichts sich regt, ____

____ nur lei - se die Hand ____ auf die Klinke ge - legt.

Mit Trit - ten, wie Trit - te der El - fen so

sacht, um ü - ber die Blu - men zu hü - pfen.

24

Nur Mut!

Op. 17 No 5

26

halb nur hei - ter, schei - dest du für im - merdar von dem Lei - - den

dem Be - glei - ter, der so lan - ge treu dir war. der so lan - ge, so

lan - ge treu ___ dir war.

Barkarole

„Mein Herz ist stumm"..

Op. 19 № 6

Andante molto tranquillo

Gesang

Piano

Mein Herz ist stumm, mein Herz ist kalt, er-starrt in des Win-ters

Ei-se; bis-wei-len in sei-ner Tie-fe nur wallt und zit-tert

und regt sich's lei-se, lei-se. Dann ist's, als ob ein mil--des

Tau'n die Dek-ke des Fro-stes bre-che; durch

con Ped.

34

35

„All mein Gedanken"...

Op. 21 № 1

„Du meines Herzens Krönelein"

Op. 21 Nº 2

Du mei-nes Her-zens Krö-ne-lein, du bist von lau-trem Gol - de,
wenn an - de-re da - ne-ben sein, dann bist du noch viel hol - de. Die
an - dern tun so gern ge-scheut, du _____ bist gar sanft und stil - le, dass
je - des Herz sich dein er-freut, dein Glück ist's, nicht dein Wil - le.

Die an-dern su-chen Lieb und Gunst mit tau - send fal-schen Wor-ten, du ___
___ oh - ne Mund= und Au - gen-kunst bist wert an al-len Or - ten.
Du bist, als wie die Ros' im Wald, sie weiss nichts ___ von ih-rer Blü - te, doch je-dem, der vor-
ü - ber-wallt, er - freut ___ sie das Ge - mü - te.

„Ach Lieb, ich muss nun scheiden!"

Op. 21 № 3

„Ach weh mir unglückhaftem Mann"

Op. 21 № 4

ich nicht lan-ge war-ten kann, mei-ne Schimmel woll'ns nicht lei - -

- - - den.

Ach weh mir unglückhaftem Mann, dass ich Geld und Gut nicht

hab'.

„Die Frauen sind oft fromm und still"

Op. 21 № 5

Die Frauen sind oft fromm und still, wo wir un-ge-ber-dig to-ben, und wenn sich ei-ne stär-ken will, dann blickt sie stumm nach o-ben. Ihr' Kraft und Stär-ke ist ge-ring, ein Lüftchen kann sie kni-cken, doch ist's ein eig-nes, star-kes Ding, wenn sie gen

Herrn Hans Giessen, grossherzogl. Kammersänger, freundschaftlich gewidmet

Kornblumen

Op. 22 № 1

50

Herrn Hans Giessen, grossherzogl. Kammersänger, freundschaftlich gewidmet

Mohnblumen

Op. 22 № 2

kreuz - fi - de - len,　tanz - nim - mer - mü - den See - - len;

die un - term La - chen wei - - nen　und nur ge -

bo - ren scheinen, die Korn - blumen zu ne - cken, und dennoch oft verstecken

die weichsten, be - sten Her - - zen,　im Schling - gewächs von

Epheu

Op. 22 Nº 3

an der er-sten Lieb'—um-ran-kung. hängt ihr gan-zes

Le——bensschicksal. denn sie zäh——len zu den

selt——nen Blu-men, die nur ein———mal

blü-hen.

Herrn Hans Giessen, grossherzogl. Kammersänger, freundschaftlich gewidmet

Wasserrose

Op. 22 Nº 4

Kennst du die Blu-me, die

mär-chen-haf-te, sa-gen-ge-fei-er-te Was-ser-ro-se?

Sie wiegt auf ä-the-rischem, schlan-ken Schafte das durchsichtge

So blüht   sie,   die zaubrische Schwester der Ster - ne, um-

schwärmt ___ von der träu-me-risch dunklen Pha-lä - - ne, die am

Ran-de des Teichs sich seh - - net   von   fer - - ne, und sie

nim - - mer er - reicht wie sehr sie sich   seh - ne.

Was - ser ro - se, so nenn' ich die schlan-ke, nachtlock'ge Maid, a - la-ba-stern von Wan - gen, in dem Au - ge der ah - nen-de tie-fe Ge - dan - ke, als sei sie ein Geist und auf Er-den ge - fan - gen. Wenn sie

spricht, ist's wie sil - - ber-nes Wo - gen-rau - schen,

sehr ruhig

wenn sie schweigt, ___ ist's die ah-nen-de Stil - - le der

ppp

Mond - nacht; sie scheint mit den Ster - nen Blicke zu

tau - schen, de-ren Spra-che die gleiche Na - tur sie ge -

espressivo

wohnt macht; du kannst nie er-

mü - den ins Aug' ihr zu

schau'n, das die seid - ne, lan - ge Wim-per um-

säumt — hat, und du glaubst, wie be-

64

Frühlingsgedränge

Op. 26 №1

Ruhe, meine Seele!

Op. 27 № 1

Heimliche Aufforderung

Op. 27 No 3

Morgen!

Op. 27 № 4

-nen in-mit-ten die-ser son - nen-at - men-den Er - de... und zu demStrand,dem wei -

- ten, wo-gen-blau - en, wer-den wir still und lang-sam nie-der-stei-gen,

immer ruhig

stumm wer-den wir uns in die Au - gen schauen, und auf uns sinkt des

Glük-kes stum-mes Schwei - gen....

Traum durch die Dämmerung

Op. 29 Nº 1

geh' ich hin zu der schön - sten Frau,

weit ü - ber Wie - sen im Däm - mer-grau, tief_____ in den

Busch von Jas - min. Durch Däm - mer-grau in der

Lie - be Land; ich ge - he nicht schnell, ich ei - le nicht; mich

„Ich trage meine Minne"

Sehnsucht

Op. 32 № 2

Nicht zu langsam

Gesang

Piano

pp

Con Ped.

Ich ging den Weg ent-lang, der ein - sam lag, den stets al - lein ich ge - he je - den Tag. Die Hei-de schweigt, das Feld ist menschenleer, der Wind nur webt im Knickbusch vor mir

lacht wie ei - ne Son - - ne mir in schwerer Nacht, ich zö - ge

rasch dein sü - ßes Herz an mich und flüst' - - - - re lei-se dir: ich lie -

- - - - - - be dich.

Liebeshymnus

O süsser Mai!

Op. 32 No 4

92

Pil - - - - ger, der in die - sen Gau'n ent - rann dein

Eis - hauch win - ter - li - cher Zeit, er - kor ein

Mäd - chen, mild___ wie du zu schau - - en,

lenz - frisch gleich dir in keu - - - scher Herr - lich - keit.

Himmelsboten

(Aus „des Knaben Wunderhorn")

Op. 32 № 5

96

fahrt_ vor ihr Schlaf-käm-mer-lein, weckt leis die sü - ße Lieb - ste mein, ver-

(nicht schleppen) *(non ritard.)*

(gleichsam wie mit einer Verbeugung)

kün-det ihr, was ich euch sag':_ Mein Dienst, mein Gruß,_ ein' gu - - ten

Tag. Doch müßt ihr sie fein züch - tig wek-ken, da-bei mei-ne heim-li - che

Lieb' ent-dek-ken, sollt sa - gen, wie ihr Die - ner wacht so kum-mer-voll die gan - ze

con espressione
ausdrucksvoll

Das Rosenband

Op. 36 No 1

Herrn Dr. Raoul Walter, k. b. Kammersänger verehrungsvoll zugeeignet

Für funfzehn Pfennige

(Aus „ Feiner Almanach" des Knaben Wunderhorn)

Op. 36 N⁰ 2

Schrei - ber hatt, des Gelds _____ zu viel, er kauft dem Mäd -

- - chen, was _____ sie will, für fünf-zehn Pfen - ni - ge.

Er kauft ihr ei - nen Gür - - - tel schmal, der

starrt von Gold _____ wohl ü - ber - all, für fünfzehn Pfen - - ni - ge.

Herrn Dr. Raoul Walter, k.b. Kammersänger, verehrungsvoll zugeeignet

Hat gesagt_ bleibt's nicht dabei

(Aus „des Knaben Wunderhorn")

Op. 36 № 3

Nicht zu schnell

Gesang

Piano

Mein Va - ter hat ge - sagt,___ ich soll das

Kind-lein wie - gen, wie - - gen, er . will mir auf den A - bend drei

Gag-gel - ei - er sie - - den, sie - - den; siedt er mir drei,

isst er mir zwei und ich mag nicht wie - gen um ein ein - zi - ges . Ei.

Mein Mut-ter hat ge-sagt, ___ ich soll die Mägd-lein ver-ra-ten, sie

wollt mir auf den A - bend drei Vö-ge-lein bra - ten, ja bra-ten;

brat sie mir drei, isst sie mir zwei, um ein

ein-zig Vög - - lein treib' ich kein Ver-rä-te-rei.

Ich liebe dich

Op. 37 N⁰ 2

sitz.

Und irrst du ver-las-sen,

ver-bannt durch die Lan - de; mit dir durch die Gas-sen

in Ar - mut und Schan - - - de! Es

blu-ten die Hän-de die Fü - - sse sind wund,

vier trostlo - se Wän - - de, es kennt uns kein Hund.

più tranquillo
ruhiger

Steht sil - ber - be -

schla - gen dein Sarg am Al - tar, sie sol - - len mich

tra - - gen zu dir auf die Bahr, und fern auf der

114

Hai - de   und stirbst du in   Not,_____   den Dolch aus der Schei de,

dir nach _____   in den Tod!

Mein Auge

Op. 37 No 4

Herr Lenz

Op. 37 N⁰ 5

ihm Lo - - - se. Dort biegt er um das

Gie - bel-haus, die Ta-schen vol-ler Ga - ben, da strek-ken sich die

Hän-de aus, ein je - - der möch-te ei-nen Strauß— hei!— für sein Mä - -

- del ha - ben. Ich ho -

- le mir auch ei - nen Schatz____ hin-weg von Glas und Schüs - sel.

Hut auf!____ Wir ren - nen ü-bern Platz: Herr Lenz,____ für

ih - - ren Bu - sen-latz ein'n gel - ben Him - - - mels-

schlüs - sel!

Herrn Dr. Fritz Sieger freundschaftlichst gewidmet

Junghexenlied

Op. 39 № 2

der - stim - men schön.

Mir war's, ich strei-chelt' ein lin - des Haar, mir

war so weh und wun - - - - - - der-

-bar.

Da schwand das Klin-geln mit ei - nem- mal, ich sah ___ hin - un - ter in's tie - fe Thal, ___ da sah ich Licht in mei-nem Haus, ___ rack schack, scha-cke, mein Pferd ___ chen, mein

Büb - chen sah _____ nach der Mut - - - ter aus, _____

Kling-ling, _____ kling-ling, _____

kling-ling, kling-ling, klin-ge-la - lei. _____

Der Arbeitsmann

Op. 39 Nº 3

Gesang

Piano

Allegro moderato

Wir ha-ben ein Bett, wir ha-ben ein Kind, mein Weib!_____ Wir ha-ben auch Ar-

beit und gar zu zweit,_____ und ha-ben die

wuchtig

Nur Zeit!

Lied an meinen Sohn

Op. 39 № 5

auf - ge-wacht vom Sturm, _____ bis _____

_____ ei-ne gra-ue Nacht wie heu - te kam.

Dumpf bran-det heut im Forst der Föhn _____ wie da - mals, wenn ich sein Getön vor

Furcht _____ wie mei-nes Va - ters Wort _____ ver - nahm. _____

Und wenn dir einst von

Soh - nes-pflicht,_____ mein Sohn,_____ dein al - ter

Va - ter spricht,_____ ge - horch'_____ ihm

In der Campagna

Op. 41ª Nº 2

141

-ler schrei- - - -te! Wie

ist die Brust von Glück ge- -schwellt, mich um-

gau- -kelt die luf- -ti-ge Schaar meiner

Lie- - - - - -der, und ich

grü - - sse die Welt, die-se herr - - - - li - che
Welt! _____ Ich grü - - - sse sie, _____
_____ mor - - - - - - - - gen seh' ich sie
wie - - - der!

cresc.

ff
sfz

sfz
ff

Marquartstein, 24. August 1899

Am Ufer

Op. 41ª Nº 3

zau - dert nicht; _____ der

Flut ent - springt ein Stern - - - - chen,

dei - ne See - - le trinkt _____ das

ə - - - wi - ge Licht. _____

Marquartstein, 15. August 1899.

Bruder Liederlich

Op. 41ª Nº 4

Ich glau-be, sie war erst sechs- -zehn Jahr_____ trug

ro- - -the Bän- -der im schwarzen Haar und plau-der-te

wie der lu-stig-ste Staar. Hal- li und Hal- lo._____

Was hat-te das Mä-del zwei fri- sche Ba- cken, Hal- li._____

Krach, konn-ten die Zäh - ne die Ha-sel-nuss kna -cken,

Hal - lo. Sie hat mir das Zim-mer mit Blu-men ge-schmückt, die

wir auf heim - -li-chen We-gen ge-pflückt; wie hab' ich da-für an's

Herz sie ge-drückt! Hal-li und Hal - lo, Hal-li und Hal - lo.

152

Marquartstein, 16. August 1899.

An Sie

162

See - - - - - - - - - - - - - - le,

wenn sie, dass sie ge-liebt wird, trun - - ken vor

Lie - - - - be sich denkt.

Marquartstein. 14. August 1899.

„Gestern war ich Atlas"

Op. 46 № 2

166

Die sieben Siegel

Op. 46 № 3

Weil ich dich nicht le - gen kann un - ter Schloss und Rie - gel, dir zum Ab - schied leg' ich an die - se sie - ben Sie - gel.

Charlottenburg, 18. November 1894.

Ich sehe wie in einem Spiegel

Op. 46 № 5

Herrn J. C. Pflüger in Bremen freundschaftlichst gewidmet

Von den sieben Zechbrüdern

Op. 47 No 5

Es ist das gu - te Wört - lein Was - - - - - - ser, da - rin doch sonst kein Ar - ges steckt. Wie kommt's nun, dass die wil - den Pras-ser dies schlich - te Wort _ so mäch - tig schreckt? Merkt auf! ich be-rich - te die Wun-der-ge-

Immer äusserst schnell.

185

196

Charlottenburg, 11. Juni 1900.

Freundliche Vision

die - ses wei - ssen Hau - - ses, _____ in den Frie - - -

den, der voll Schön - heit war - tet, dass wir kom - - men. _____

Und ich geh' mit Ei - - ner, die mich lieb hat in den

Frie - - den voll Schön - - - - - heit!

immer ruhiger

dim.   pp

ritard.

Charlottenburg, 5. October 1900

Kling!...

Op. 48 N⁰ 3

202

auf dem ver - dorr - - - - - ten Ge - fild. _____

Kling, meine See - le, Kling! _____ kling, meine See - - -

- le, kling! Kling! Sing!

Kling! _____

Charlottenburg, 30. September 1900

Winterweihe

Op. 48 Nº 4

Das Rad der Zeit mag rol- len, wir grei - - fen kaum_ hin-

ein, demSchein der Welt ver-schol-len, auf un-serm Ei - - land wol- len wir

Tag und Nacht der sel' - - - - gen Lie - -

- be _ weihn.

Charlottenburg, 28. September 1900

Ernst Kraus gewidmet

In goldener Fülle

Op. 49 № 2

keit.

Wir schreiten in gol - de - ner

Fül - le durch se - li - ges Som - mer - land_

wir schrei - ten in gol - de - ner Fül - le_

bis an das En - de der Welt_

wir

schrei - ten in gol - - - de - ner Fül - - -

le durch al - le E - - - wig - keit.

Charlottenburg, 18.September 1901.

Herrn Consul Simon gewidmet

Das Lied des Steinklopfers

Op. 49 № 4

den und auch kein Geld. Dich will ich krie-gen,

du har-ter Plo - cken die Splitter flie-gen, der Sand stäubt

auf „Du ar - mer Fle - gel" mein Va - ter brumm-te

„Nimm' mei - nen Schlä - - gel"; und starb da - rauf.

219

Charlottenburg 24. September 1901

Meiner lieben Pauline zum 8. August 1903 gewidmet

Gefunden

Op. 56 № 1

Äug - lein — schön. Ich wollt' es bre - chen, da sagt' es fein: „Soll ich zum

Wel - ken ge - bro - chen sein?"

Ich grub's mit — al - len den Würz - lein — aus, zum

Gar - ten trug — ich's am hüb - - schen Haus.

Blindenklage

Op. 56 № 2

Mäßig schnell

Wenn ich dich ___ fra - ge, dem das Le - - ben
blüht: O sa - ge mir, sa - ge, wie das
Mohn - - feld ___ glüht! ___ Das ro - te
Mohn - - feld, wie es jauchzt und lacht: ___

Meiner lieben Mutter gewidmet

Im Spätboot

Op. 56 N⚬ 3

Frühlingsfeier

Op 56 No 5

A - do - - - - - - nis!"

238

Die heiligen drei Könige aus Morgenland

Op. 56 N⁰ 6

TRANSLATIONS OF THE TEXTS

Zueignung (Dedication)

Yes, you know it, dear soul,
That I suffer when far from you;
Love makes hearts sick;
Take my thanks.

Once, the toper of freedom,
I held aloft the amethyst goblet,
And you blessed the draught;
Take my thanks.

And you therein exorcised the evil ones,
Until I, as I had never yet been,
Fell in great sanctity upon your heart;
Take my thanks.

Nichts (Nothing)

You say I should name
My queen in the realm of song?
Fools that you are, I know
Her even less than any of you do.

Ask me about the color of her eyes,
Ask me about the sound of her voice,
Ask me about her walk and dancing and posture,
Alas, and what do I know of it?

Is the sun not the source
Of all life, of all light?
And what is known about it
By me, by you, by anyone? Nothing.

Die Nacht (The Night)

Out of the forest steps the night,
Out of the trees it slips softly,
Looks around in a wide circle;
Now be careful.

All the lights of this world,
All flowers, all colors
Night extinguishes, and steals the sheaves
Out of the field.

It takes everything in which we delight,
Takes away the silver of the stream,
Takes away the gold from the copper roof
Of the cathedral.

The bushes stand despoiled;
Come closer, soul to soul;
Oh, I fear that the night will steal
You from me too.

Allerseelen (All Souls' Day)

Place the fragrant mignonettes on the table,
Bring over the last red asters,
And let us speak of love again,
As once in May.

Give me your hand, so I can squeeze it secretly,
And if people see, it's all the same to me;
Give me just one of your sweet glances,
As once in May.

Flowers bloom fragrantly on every grave today;
Indeed, one day in the year is spared for the dead;
Come to my heart, so I can have you again,
As once in May.

Madrigal

I humbly bend my neck to the yoke,
I bow this head, smiling in the face of misfortune,
This heart, which loves and believes,
In the face of her who is my enemy.

Against this pain I do not protest grudgingly;
Rather, I fear that it may someday diminish.
If the beam of your eyes
Has transformed this sorrow into the sap of life,
What sorrow then has the power to kill me?

I humbly bend my neck to the yoke [etc.]

Winternacht (Winter Night)

With rain and the rumble of storm,
I welcome you, month of December;
Lead me on the path to the cozy house
In which my beloved lady lives.

Never have I greeted the blossoms of May,
The sky growing blue, the gleaming dew
As happily as today I greet your snowfall,
Your brew of mist and grayness of clouds;

For, through the tumult of the snowflakes,
More beautifully than any spring has laughed,
There shines and blossoms the springtime of love
Secretly for me now in the winter night.

Heimkehr (Return Home)

The boughs wave more gently,
The boat races toward the shore,
The dove returns home to its nest,
My heart returns home to you.

Sufficiently now, in the glittering daylight,
When the hubbub of life is heard all around,
It has roamed into the distance
With a wandering beat of wings.

But now that the sun has departed,
And silence descends upon the grove,
It feels: peace dwells with you,
Repose with you alone.

Ständchen (Serenade)

Open the door, open the door, but quietly, my dear,
So as not to awaken anyone from slumber.
The brook barely murmurs, barely does a leaf
On the bushes and hedges tremble in the wind.
And so, quietly, my darling, so that no one stirs,
Just place your hand gently on the handle.

With steps as light as the steps with which elves
Hop over the flowers,
Fly softly out into the moonlit night,
To slip into the garden and meet me.
All round, the blossoms slumber by the babbling
brook
And emit fragrance in their sleep; only love is
awake.

Sit down, there is a mysterious half-light here
Under the lime trees;
The nightingale above our head shall

Dream about our kisses,
And the rose, when it awakes in the morning,
Shall glow brightly from the night's shudders of
ecstasy.

Nur Mut! (Be Brave!)

Abandon your timidity, bear courageously
Your worries, your pain;
No matter how bloody the wound is,
It will still heal someday.

Beneath a thick blanket of ice
The young bud is already dreaming
That the springtime is awakening it
With the pleasant sound of songs.

Just turn your gaze upward,
And through the gloomy gray of the clouds
There will finally break, so as to dazzle you,
The blue of the sky, gloriously.

But even the sad hours
And the tears that you weep,
Believe me, will someday seem sweeter to you,
Like joys that have vanished.

And with melancholy, only half-cheerful,
You will part forever
With your suffering, the companion
That was faithful to you for so long.

Barkarole (Barcarolle)

Around the tips of the sinking oars
Trembles and gleams a shimmering brightness,
And with every stroke it flies like lightning flashes
Dancing from wave to wave.

In my breast, with the raptures of love,
My heart trembles and gleams like the water,
Shouts exultantly to the stars and suns,
Trembles to perish in the surging flames.

Already on the cliff, through the green of the plane
trees,
I see the roof supported on columns,
And the wavering light on the terrace
Informs me that my beloved is still awake.

Fly, my boat, and shelter us discreetly,
Shelter us, blessed August night;
Yes, it is sweet to rock upon the waves,
But sweeter upon her breast.

"Mein Herz ist stumm" (My Heart Is Mute)

My heart is mute, my heart is cold,
Grown rigid in the winter's ice;
Only from time to time, deep down, it moves
And trembles and gently stirs.

At such time a gentle thaw seems to be
Breaking the cover of the frost;
Through woods growing green, blooming
    meadows,
The brooks murmur again.

And the sound of horns, borne from leaf to leaf
By the spring wind,
Bursts from the glens and reaches my ear softly,
Like a call from blissful days.

But my aging heart will no longer grow young,
The echo of the dying sound
Comes from an ever-increasing distance,
And everything is frozen again.

My heart is mute, my heart is cold.

"All mein Gedanken" (All My Thoughts)

All my thoughts, my heart and my mind
Travel to where my sweetheart is.
They make their way despite walls and gates;
Then no bolts, no ditches obstruct them;
They go high in the air like the birds,
They need no bridges over rivers and ravines,
They find the town and they find the house,
They single out her window from all the others.
And they knock and call: "Open up, let us in,
We come from your loved one and we greet you
    sweetly,
Open up, open up, let us in."

"Du meines Herzens Krönelein" (You, the Crown of My Heart)

You, the crown of my heart,
You are of pure gold;
When others are beside you,
Then you are much fairer.

The others like to act so smart,
You are very gentle and quiet;
The fact that every heart rejoices in you
Is your good fortune, not something you have
    willed.

The others seek love and favor
With a thousand false words,
You, without art of lips or eyes,
Are worthy everywhere.

You are like the rose in the woods,
It knows nothing of its bloom,
But it gives joy to the spirit
Of everyone who passes by.

"Ach Lieb, ich muss nun scheiden!" (Oh, Love, I Now Must Part)

Oh, love, I now must part,
Must go over mountain and valley;
The alders and the willows
Are all weeping.

They saw us so often walking
Together by the edge of the brook;
One of us without the other
Is beyond their understanding.

The alders and the willows
Are in tears with grief;
Now imagine how the two of us
Must feel in our hearts.

"Ach weh mir unglückhaftem Mann" (Oh, Woe Is Me, Unfortunate Man)

Oh, woe is me, unfortunate man,
That I don't have money or property,
Otherwise I would immediately harness four white
    horses
And ride over to you at a trot.
I would adorn them with jingle bells,
So you would hear me from a distance,
I would put a big bouquet of roses
At my left side.
And when I came to your little house,
I would crack my whip;
Then you would peep out of the window:
"What do you want?" you would ask.
"What is the big bouquet of roses for,
The white horses pulling the carriage?"
"I want *you*," I would call; "come out!"
Then you wouldn't raise a single question.
"Now, Father, Mother, look at her
And kiss her goodbye quickly,
Because I can't wait long,
My white horses won't abide it."
Oh, woe is me, unfortunate man,
That I don't have money or property.

"Die Frauen sind oft fromm und still" (Women are
    Often Pious and Quiet)

Women are often pious and quiet
When we men rage in unruly fashion,
And when one of them wants to strengthen
    herself,
She looks upward silently.
Their force and strength are slight,
A breeze can break them in two,
But it's a peculiar, mighty thing
When they look up to heaven.
I've often looked upward myself
When my mother looked up that way;
I saw only gray clouds passing
And blue sky up there;
But she, when she looked down again,
Was full of strength and hope;
It seems to me that women now and then
Still see heaven exposed to view.

Kornblumen (Cornflowers)

I call "cornflowers" those women
Who are gentle and have blue eyes,
Who, undemanding in their still ways,
Impart the dew of peace, which they absorb

From their own clear souls,
To everyone that they approach,
Unaware of the jewels of feeling
That they receive from a heavenly hand.

You feel as good in their presence
As if you were walking through a field of grain
Through which the evening breeze was blowing,
Full of pious peace and full of gentleness.

Mohnblumen (Poppy Flowers)

"Poppy flowers" are the round,
Red-blooded, healthy,
Freckled and tanned,
Always cheerful,
Good-as-gold, merry-as-a-cricket,
Never-tired-of-dancing souls;
Who cry while they laugh
And seem born only
To tease the "cornflowers,"
And yet often conceal
The softest, kindest hearts

In the creeping plants of their jokes;
Whom, God knows, you would have to
Smother with kisses,
If you weren't always afraid
That if you embraced the minx,
She would burst apart in a blaze,
Like a fully laden fireship!

Epheu (Ivy)

But I call "ivy" the girls
With the soft words,
With the plain bright hair
Around their lightly curved foreheads,
With the brown, soulful doe's eyes
That are so often full of tears,
And when tearful are particularly irresistible;
Without strength or self-consciousness,
Unadorned, with hidden blossom,
But with an inexhaustibly deep,
Loyal, heartfelt feeling,
They can never with their own strength
Raise themselves from their roots;
They are born to twine
Lovingly around another living thing:
The fate of their entire life
Depends on their first amorous entwinement,
For they are among the rare flowers
That bloom only once.

Wasserrose (Water Lily)

Do you know the flower, the fairy-tale-like
Water lily, celebrated in legend?
It waves its transparent, colorless head
On an ethereal, slender stem;

It blooms in a reedy pond in the grove,
Guarded by the swan, who solitarily encircles it,
It opens only in the moonlight,
With which it has its silvery shimmer in common:

Thus it blooms, the magical sister of the stars,
Adored by the dreamily dark moth,
Which longs for it from afar at the edge of the
    pond,
But never reaches it, yearn as it may.

"Water lily" is what I call the slender
Maid with tresses of night, with alabaster cheeks,

The presentient, deep thought in her eyes,
As if she were a spirit and a prisoner on earth.

When she speaks, it's like the silvery murmur of
    waves;
When she is silent, it's the presentient silence of the
    moonlit night;
She seems to exchange glances with the stars,
To whose language her similar nature makes her
    accustomed;

You can never grow tired of looking into her eyes,
Which are edged with long, silky lashes,
And you believe, as if spellbound by blissful dread,
All that the Romantic Era dreamed about fairies.

Frühlingsgedränge (Springtime Throng)

Children of the spring in a colorful throng,
Fluttering flowers, fragrant breaths,
Languishing, jubilant songs of love
Fling themselves at my heart from every bush.

Children of the spring hover about my heart,
Whisper into it with flattering words,
Call into it with an intoxicated hubbub,
Shake long-locked doors.

Children of the spring, surrounding my heart,
What are you seeking there so urgently?
Did I reveal it to you recently while dreaming,
Slumbering under a blossoming tree?

Did morning winds bring you the report
That I have locked in my heart
Your lovely playmate,
And secretly and happily bear her portrait?

Ruhe, meine Seele! (Rest, My Soul!)

Not a breeze gently stirs;
Fallen into gentle slumber, the grove reposes;
Through the dark covering of the leaves
Bright sunshine steals.

Rest, rest, my soul,
Your storms passed wildly,
You have raged and you have trembled,
Like the surf when it swells.

These times are powerful,
They distress heart and brain—
Rest, rest, my soul,
And forget what threatens you!

Heimliche Aufforderung (Secret Invitation)

Up, raise the glistening goblet to your lips,
And at this festive meal drink till your heart is
    whole.
And when you raise it, give me a secret signal,
Then I'll smile and then I'll drink quietly like
    you . . .

And quietly, like me, observe around us the host
Of drunken prattlers—don't despise them too
    badly.
No, raise the gleaming goblet, filled with wine,
And let them be happy at their noisy meal.

But once you have enjoyed the meal, quenched
    your thirst,
Then abandon the merry picture of our loud
    companions,
And walk out into the garden to the rosebush,
Where I will await you then in accordance with our
    old custom,

And I shall fall on your bosom, before you expect
    it,
And drink your kisses, as often in the past,
And braid the splendor of the roses into your hair.
Oh, come, you wonderful, longed-for night!

Morgen! (Tomorrow!)

And tomorrow the sun will shine again
And on the path that I shall follow
It will reunite us, fortunate ones,
In the midst of this sunshine-breathing earth . . .

And to the beach, wide and blue with waves,
We shall descend, silently and slowly;
Mutely we shall look into each other's eyes,
And the mute silence of happiness shall descend
    upon us . . .

Traum durch die Dämmerung (Dream in the Twilight)

Broad meadows in the gray of twilight;
The sun's light has gone out, the stars are arriving;
Now I go to meet the most beautiful woman,
Far over meadows in the gray of twilight,
Deep into the jasmine bushes.

Through the gray of twilight into the land of love,
I do not walk fast, I do not hasten;
A soft, velvet cord draws me
Through the gray of twilight into the land of love,
Into a blue, gentle light.

"Ich trage meine Minne" (I Carry My Love)

I carry my love—
Mute with rapture—
Around with me in my heart
And my mind.

Yes, that I found you,
You dear girl,
That will give me joy all the days
That are allotted to me.

And even if the sky is gloomy
And the night coal-black,
Brightly shines the sunny-gold splendor
Of my love.

And even if the world lies in sin,
And it pains me,
The evil world must be dazzled
By the snow of your innocence.

Sehnsucht (Longing)

I went along the path that lay solitary,
The one I travel alone, every day.
The heath is silent, the field is empty of people,
Only the wind blows by in the brush in front of
    me.

The road lies far extended in front of me,
My heart has longed only for you.
And if you came, it would be a miracle for me;
I would bow before you: "I love you."

And as we met, only a single glance—
It would be the destiny of my whole life.
And if you looked coldly upon me,
I would defy you, girl: "I love you!"

But if your beautiful eyes greeted me and smiled,
Like a sun in my heavy night,
I would quickly draw your sweet heart to myself
And would quietly whisper to you: "I love you."

Liebeshymnus (Hymn of Love)

Bless the day that gave you birth,
Bless the one on which I first saw you!
Lost in the brightness of your eyes
I stand, a blissful dreamer.

It seems to me that that heaven is opening
Of which I had merely a distant presentiment,
And I am permitted to view a sun
At which my longing merely hinted.

How beautiful my image in this glance!
In this glance, how great my good fortune!
And beseechingly I call to destiny:
"Oh, remain, remain without changing!"

O süsser Mai! (Oh, Sweet May!)

Oh, sweet May, oh, be merciful;
Oh, sweet May, I beseech you warmly:
I see the fields growing warm on your bosom,
And everything that lives beneath your spell is
    growing;
You who are so gentle and endlessly gracious,
Oh, dear May, grant me the gift!

The gloomy pilgrim who in these regions
Escaped the icy breath of the winter season
Has chosen a girl, as gentle to behold as you are,
Fresh as spring, like you, in her chaste splendor.
That we may love and embrace each other lovingly,
Mercy, May, most lovely one, mercy!

Himmelsboten (Heavenly Messengers)

The moonlight has already paled,
The dark night has crept away;
Arise, you noble dawn,
All my trust is in you.

Phoebus, its well-adorned forerunner,
Has already prepared his chariot,
The sun's steeds are harnessed to it,
The reins are in his hand.

Its forerunner, Don Lucifer,
Already hovers in the sky,
He has opened up the clouds
And watered the earth with his dew.

Oh, go to her little bedroom,
Gently awaken my sweet beloved,
Report to her what I tell you,
My service, my greeting, a good day.

But you must awaken her respectably,
And, doing so, reveal my secret love;
You are to tell her how her servant lies awake
All night so feverishly.

Look at her yellow hair for me,
Her white neck, her clear eyes;
Kiss her red lips for me,
And, if she allows it, her round breasts.

Das Rosenband (The Cord of Roses)

I found her in the springtime shade,
Then I bound her with cords of roses:
She did not feel it but slumbered on.

I looked at her; with that glance
My life hung on her life:
I surely felt it but did not know.

But I murmured to her soundlessly
And rustled the cords of roses:
Then she awoke from her slumber.

She looked at me: with that glance
Her life hung on my life:
And all around us it became Elysium.

Für funfzehn Pfennige (For Fifteen Cents)

The girl wants to have a suitor,
Even if she has to dig him out of the ground—
For fifteen cents.

She dug in, she dug out,
And dug out only a clerk—
For fifteen cents.

The clerk had too much money,
He bought the girl anything she wanted—
For fifteen cents.

He bought her a narrow belt,
Stiff with gold all over—
For fifteen cents.

He bought her a wide hat
That would be good for the sun—
For fifteen cents.

CLERK:
Good for the sun, good for the wind,
Stay with me, my dear girl—
For fifteen cents.

If you stay with me, I'll stay with you;
I'll give you everything I possess—
It's fifteen cents.

GIRL:
Keep your property, leave me my spirits;
After all, no other woman will take you—
For fifteen cents.

CLERK:
Your high spirits, I don't want them;
You surely have no faithful love—
For fifteen cents.

Your heart is like a dovecote:
One man goes in, the other comes out—
For fifteen cents.

Hat gesagt—bleibt's nicht dabei (He Said So, But That Won't Be the End of It)

My father said I should rock the baby,
He'd boil three hen's eggs for me in the evening;
If he boils three for me,
He'll eat two on me,
And I don't want to rock the baby for a single egg.

My mother said I should tattle on the girls,
She'd roast three birds for me in the evening;
If she roasts three for me,
She'll eat two on me,
And I won't be a tattler for a single bird.

My sweetheart said I should think of him,
He'd give me three kisses in the evening;
If he gives me three,
That won't be the end of it,
What do I care about the bird, what's the egg to me?

Ich liebe dich (I Love You)

Four noble steeds
In front of our carriage,
We live in the palace
In proud comfort.

The waves of morning light
And then the lightning—
All that they illuminate
Is our property.

And if you wander forsaken,
In exile through many lands,
I shall go with you through the alleys
In poverty and shame!

Our hands bleed,
Our feet are sore,
Four cheerless walls,
Not a dog knows us.

When your coffin, covered with silver,
Is placed beside the altar,
Let them carry me
To your bier.

And far away on the heath,
Should you die in want,
I shall draw my dagger from its sheath
And follow you in death!

Mein Auge (My Eyes)

You are my eyes! You penetrate me fully,
You have illuminated my entire being,
Filled my whole life with brightness,
Brought me, when I was stumbling, onto a safe
    path!

My eyes, you! How blind I really was
In heart and mind before you became my
    companion,
And now how the resplendence of this whole
    world
Flows through me, so brightly and mildly
    transfigured!
You are my eyes, you!

Herr Lenz (Mr. Springtime)

Today Mr. Springtime is leaping through the town
In blue trousers.
And all those who have two young legs
Leap because the rising sap makes them happy,
    leap because they are sated with sunshine,
And buy lottery tickets from him.

There he is turning the corner of the gabled house,
His pockets full of presents;
Then people hold out their hands,
Every man would like to have a bouquet,
Hurrah! for his girl.

I get hold of a sweetheart, too,
Pulling her away from the glasses and dishes.
Put on your hat! We're running to the square!
Mr. Springtime, as a corsage for her
Let me have a yellow primrose!

Junghexenlied (Young Witch's Song)

When at night I rode over the mountains,
Clippity-clop, my little horse,
A strange ringing rode along,
Ding-a-ling, ding-a-ling.

It was a wheedlingly beseeching sound,
It was as beautiful as children's voices.
I felt as if I were stroking soft hair,
I felt so pained and unusual.

Then the ringing disappeared all at once,
I looked down into the deep valley,
Then I saw light in my house.
Clippity-clop, my little horse,
My little boy was looking out to see his mother,
Ding-a-ling, ding-a-ling.

Der Arbeitsmann (The Worker)

We have a bed, we have a child,
My wife!
We also have work, and indeed together,
And have the sun and rain and wind,
And we're lacking only a trifle
To be as free as the birds are:
Only time.

When we walk through the fields on Sundays,
My child,
And see the blue tribe of swallows flashing
Far and wide over the stalks of grain,
Oh, it's not the bit of clothing we then lack
To be as beautiful as the birds are:
Only time.

Only time! We scent a stormwind,
We common folk!
Only a small eternity;
For we lack nothing, my wife, my child,
Except all that thrives through our efforts,
To be as happy as the birds are:
Only time.

Lied an meinen Sohn (Song to My Son)

The storm is eavesdropping on my home,
My heart is beating out into the night,
Loudly; even when still a child I would be
    awakened
This way by the noises of the forest.
My young son, listen, listen:
Piercing the remote repose of your cradle,
The wind is moaning my words to you in your
    dream.

Once I too laughed in my sleep,
My son, and was not awakened
By the storm—
Until a gray night like this one came.
Tonight the mountain wind is surging hollowly in
    the forest
Just like then, when I heard its sounds
Out of fear, as if they were my father's words.

Hear how the budding row of treetops
Is writhing and bending, from tree to tree;
My son, into the repose of your cradle
The storm laughs angrily: listen, listen!
It has never bent in fear;
Hear how it blows sharply through the treetops:
Be yourself! Be yourself!

And when someday your old father speaks
To you, my son, about a son's obligations,

Don't heed him, don't heed him:
Hear how the mountain wind in the forest is
      preparing the springtime!
Listen, it is eavesdropping on my home,
My heart is beating out into the night,
Loudly.

In der Campagna (In the Campagna)

I greet the sun that is setting there,
I greet the silent waves of the sea
That thirstily, thirstily drinks the flames
That noiselessly bleed to death on its bosom.

I greet the plain—how still it lies—
The mysteriously dusky extent of the evening,
Through which I, in my desire to return home,
Now stride more and more quickly!

How my breast swells with happiness;
The airy throng of my songs hovers around me,
And I greet the world, this wonderful world!
I say goodnight to it, tomorrow I shall see it again!

Am Ufer (On the Shore)

The world falls silent, your blood begins to
      resound,
Into its bright abyss sinks
The faroff day, it does not tremble;
The blaze engulfs
The highest stretch of land, in the sea
The faroff night struggles, it does not tarry;
From the waters there springs
A little star, your soul drinks
The eternal light.

Bruder Liederlich (Mr. Scapegrace)

A feather on my helmet in sports and dangers,
Halli.
I never in my life learned how to fast or be thrifty,
Hallo.
I don't let girls pass by freely,
Where men are brawling there you'll find me,
And where they're swilling, I swill for three.
Halli and hallo.

Damn! A girl has remained in my memory,
Halli.
I can't force her out of my heart,
Hallo.

I think she was no more than sixteen,
Wore red ribbons in her black hair
And chattered like the merriest starling.
Halli and hallo.

Did that girl have two bright cheeks!
Halli.
Crunch! how her teeth could crack hazelnuts!
Hallo.
She decorated my room with flowers
That we had picked on secret paths;
How I pressed her to my heart in thanks!
Halli and hallo.

We passed the time marvelously,
Halli.
I wanted us to stay together,
Hallo.
But the affair started to bore me no end,
I told her that the government had appointed me
To buy camels in Samarkand.
Halli and hallo.

And when I gave my darling my hand to say
      goodbye,
Halli,
She started to weep bitterly,
Hallo.
Why is it that just today I remember constantly
How roughly I gave her her walking papers . . .
Bring me wine, damn it! and there's my trump ace!
Halli and hallo.

An Sie (To Her)

Time, announcer of the best joys,
Approach, blessed time;
To seek you out in faraway places
I shed too many depressing tears.

And yet you are coming! Oh, yes, angels are
      sending you,
You are sent to me by angels,
Who were once people, who once loved as I do,
And now love as an immortal loves.

On the wings of repose, in the morning breezes,
Bright with the dew of the day
That smiles while rising, with the eternal
Springtime you descend the sky.

For, the full soul feels itself complete and pours
      rapture
In the heart,
When, drunk with love,
It reflects that it is loved.

"Gestern war ich Atlas" (Yesterday I Was Atlas)

Yesterday I was Atlas, who bore the heavens,
When my darling's heart beat against my bosom;
The suns of her eyes circled over me
And her breath sported around me like the aether.

Oh, pull the knot of love even more tightly!
As long as I've been breathing, I have not yet found
    peace.
Let me breathe freely joined with you! I feel a lack
As long as I am still something other than you.

For me the longer your kiss is, the better;
For me the tighter your embrace is, the better;
To be sure, your long kiss alarms me,
But the more alarmed I am, the better.

Die sieben Siegel (The Seven Seals)

Because I cannot place you
Under lock and key,
On parting, I place on you
These seven seals.

Kisses shall be seals,
One on the lips,
So that no honey-thief
Can sip from my goblet of nectar!

This seal on your bosom,
This on your neck;
May the desires of outsiders be far from the
    pleasure
Of my paradise!

Two more on cheek and cheek,
And on eye and eye,
So that no mouth longs for them,
And no glances drink them in!

Dear child, for your fault
Wear the seals patiently!
Tomorrow we shall once more
Undo the nasty seven seals.

Ich sehe wie in einem Spiegel (As in a Mirror I See)

As in a mirror I see
Myself in my darling's eyes;
I am freed of every seal
That concealed my own self from me.

Through your gaze my heart and the world
Have become transparent to me;

What is real in the world and what is trivial
Has been eternally clarified for me.

Just as the quiet beat of your heart
Passes through my breast here,
So I feel what moves the universe
From the day of creation until doomsday.

All the worlds revolve around love;
Love is their life, love is their death;
And within me there surges a world-process
Of love's pleasure and love's distress.

The soul of the creation is eternal peace,
Its life-spirit is a constant war.
And so peace falls to my lot,
Victory over death and life, victory!

I speak quietly to the love in my heart,
As flowers speak to the sunshine:
Give me pleasure, give me sorrows!
I live and die belonging to you!

Von den sieben Zechbrüdern (Of the Seven Drinking Companions)

I know seven jolly brothers,
They're the thirstiest men in town;
They swore up and down, never again
To utter a certain word,
Not in any way,
Neither loudly nor softly.

It's the fine little word "water,"
In which ther's usually no harm.
How is it, then, that this simple word
So greatly frightens the wild rakes?
Pay attention! I shall narrate
The strange story.

Once those thirsty seven heard
From a toper they didn't know
That up there in the wooded mountains
A new inn had opened
In which there flowed such pure,
Tasty wines.

For the sake of a good sermon
None of them would have budged from the spot;
But when it's a question of filling glasses properly,
The fellows are immediately excited.
"Come, let's head there!"
One calls to another.

In the morning they set out heartily;
Soon the sun climbs higher, oppressively hot;
Their tongues are parched, their lips burn,

And from their forehead the sweat streams down.
There from the cliffs
The brook babbles so brightly.

How they drink in long draughts!
But barely have they quenched their thirst,
When they declare their discontentment
That no wine, but only water, flows here:
"Oh, insipid drink!
Oh, pitiful rinsing fluid!"

The forest now draws the pilgrims
Into its highly complex paths;
There they suddenly stand still, in a fix:
Tangled thickets block their way.
They go astray, they seek,
They quarrel and curse.

Meanwhile the sultry sun has become
Deeply enveloped in dark storms;
The rain is already rattling through the leaves,
Lightning flashes, thunder roars;
Then it comes down in buckets,
An unending downpour.

Soon the forest becomes a thousand islands,
Numberless streams burst forth;
Here no raging helps, here no whining helps,
The noble chorus must get through.
Oh, the thorough baptism!
Oh, the wonderful shower-bath!

In ancient times human beings
Were often transformed into fountains and rivers;
Our seven poor sinners, too,
Are threatened by a similar decision of the gods.
They drip, they swell up,
As if they were fountains.

And so, swimming more than walking,
They manage to get out of the forest;
But they see no splendid inn,
They are on the direct road home.
Already from the cliffs
The brook babbles so brightly.

Then it seems to be saying as it murmurs:
"Welcome, my fine band of brothers!
Insolent fools, you disdained
My water, which refreshed you.
Now you are soaked,
So you can remember it!"

That's how it came about that the seven brothers
Feared water from then on,
And that they swore never again
To utter the accursed word,
Not in any way,
Neither loudly nor softly.

Freundliche Vision (Friendly Vision)

I didn't dream this while sleeping,
I saw it lovely before me in broad daylight.
A meadow full of daisies;
A white house deep in green bushes;
Statues of gods gleam from the foliage.
And I walk with a woman who loves me,
With a calm spirit, into the coolness
Of this white house, into the peace
That, full of beauty, awaits our coming.

Kling! . . . (Ring! . . .)

Ring! . . .
My soul emits a pure tone.
And I thought the poor thing
Was already torn by the furious grief
Of troubled times.

Sing,
My soul, the confessional song
Of recovered plenitude!
Lift the cover from your heart!
I greet you, purified inner sound!

Ring out,
My soul, your life,
Flowing, fresh image!
Blossoming has returned
To the dried-up field.

Ring, my soul, ring!

Winterweihe (Winter Consecration)

In these winter days,
Now that the light is covered,
Let us carry in our heart,
And tell each other intimately,
That which fills us with inner light.

May that which kindles a gentle glow
Burn continually;
May that which unites souls delicately,
And builds spiritual bridges,
Be our quiet slogan.

The wheel of time may turn,
We barely take part in it,
Lost to worldly illusions,
On our island we shall
Consecrate ourselves day and night to blissful love.

In goldener Fülle (In Golden Plenty)

We walk in golden plenty
Through the blessed summer land,
Our hands clasped tightly
As if joined by a magic spell.

The big summer sun
Has brightened our hearts;
We walk in golden plenty
To the very end of the world.

And when your brow contracts and grows pale,
And when my soul leaves its house,
We shall walk in golden plenty
Out into the world to come, also.

Those who are granted such a summer
Laugh at the passage of time—
We walk in golden plenty
Through all eternity.

We walk in golden plenty
Through the blessed summer land—
We walk in golden plenty
To the very end of the world—
We walk in golden plenty
Through all eternity.

Das Lied des Steinklopfers (The Song of the
    Stone Breaker)

I'm not a minister,
I'm not a king,
I'm not a priest,
I'm not a hero.
I've received no order of chivalry,
I've received no title,
Nor any money.

I'll get you,
You hard hunk of rock;
The splinters fly,
The sand rises up in a cloud—
"You poor young cub!"
My father growled—"Take my mallet";
And then he died.

Woe is me, today
I have not yet eaten a thing,
The Father of Mercy
Has sent nothing;
I have dreamt
Of golden wine, and I break stones
For the fatherland.

Not a minister, not a king, not a hero!
No orders, no titles, nor any money.
"You poor young cub," "Take my mallet,"
Eaten nothing yet, nothing sent
And break stones for the fatherland.

Gefunden (Found)

I was walking in the woods
With no particular purpose,
And it wasn't my intention
To look for anything.

In the shade I saw
A flower growing,
Shining like stars,
Beautiful as eyes.

I wanted to pick it,
When it said sweetly:
"Shall I be picked
And fade away?"

I dug it out
With all its roots,
I carried it to the garden
At the pretty house.

And replanted it
In a quiet spot;
Now it continues to branch
And keeps on blossoming.

Blindenklage (Blind Man's Lament)

If I ask you, you for whom life is blossoming,
Oh, tell me, tell me how the poppy field glows!
The red poppy field, how it exults and laughs:
My path is dead and my night everlasting.
Yes, many a misfortune strikes people a heavy
    blow;
A man who bears so much knows no more sorrow.
He zigzags blindly across sunlit meadows
And gropes for traces that have been covered over.
I dream of suns, stretch out my hand,
I want to touch things beyond the dark wall,
I want to pass the layer of shadow and grasp
Red poppies and golden rays of light . . .
A glimmer still flashes from olden days,
In the dead eyes longing remained awake,
And, knowing of the splendor of the light,

I walk through night and nothingness, thus totally
    disinherited.
Whether joy or sorrow encounters my paths,
My curse is dead and dead, too, is my blessing.

Im Spätboot (In the Late Boat)

I make the ship's bench my pillow.
Finally my hot brow becomes cool!
Oh, how sweetly my heart is growing cold!
Oh, how gently pleasure and pain are growing
    silent!
Above me, the black smoke of the funnel
Rocks and bends in the breath of the wind.
Here and there from time to time
The boat stops at many small ports:
In the sparse light of the ship's lantern
A shadow departs and no one comes on board.
Only the steersman is still awake and on his feet!
Only the wind, which blows in my hair!
Pain and pleasure undergo a quiet death.
The dark boat carries a slumberer.

Frühlingsfeier (Spring Celebration)

This is the sad pleasure of springtime!
The blossoming girls, the wild throng,
Dash by with streaming hair
And howls of sorrow and bared breasts:
"Adonis! Adonis!"

Night falls. By torchlight
They seek here and there in the forest,
Which, fear-entangled, reechoes
With weeping and laughing, with sobbing and
    shouting:
"Adonis! Adonis!"

The marvelously handsome youth
Lies on the ground pale and dead.
His blood dyes all the flowers red.
And the sound of lamentation fills the air:
"Adonis! Adonis!"

Die heiligen drei Könige aus Morgenland (The
    Three Wise Men of the East)

The Three Wise Men [holy kings] of the East
Asked in every small town:
"Which is the way to Bethlehem,
Dear boys and girls?"

The young and the old didn't know;
The Wise Men moved on;
They followed a golden star,
Which shone, lovely and serene.

The star came to a halt over Joseph's house,
They went in;
The ox bellowed, the baby cried out,
The Three Wise Men sang.

THE SIX BRANDENBURG CONCERTOS AND THE FOUR ORCHESTRAL SUITES IN FULL SCORE, Johann Sebastian Bach. Complete standard Bach-Gesellschaft editions in large, clear format. Study score. 273pp. 9 × 12.   23376-6 Pa. **$10.95**

COMPLETE CONCERTI FOR SOLO KEYBOARD AND ORCHESTRA IN FULL SCORE, Johann Sebastian Bach. Bach's seven complete concerti for solo keyboard and orchestra in full score from the authoritative Bach-Gesellschaft edition. 206pp. 9 × 12.   24929-8 Pa. **$9.95**

THE THREE VIOLIN CONCERTI IN FULL SCORE, Johann Sebastian Bach. Concerto in A Minor, BWV 1041; Concerto in E Major, BWV 1042; and Concerto for Two Violins in D Minor, BWV 1043. Bach-Gesellschaft edition. 64pp. 9⅜ × 12¼.   25124-1 Pa. **$5.95**

GREAT ORGAN CONCERTI, OPP. 4 & 7, IN FULL SCORE, George Frideric Handel. 12 organ concerti composed by great Baroque master are reproduced in full score from the *Deutsche Handelgesellschaft* edition. 138pp. 9⅜ × 12¼.   24462-8 Pa. **$7.95**

COMPLETE CONCERTI GROSSI IN FULL SCORE, George Frideric Handel. Monumental Opus 6 Concerti Grossi, Opus 3 and "Alexander's Feast" Concerti Grossi—19 in all—reproduced from most authoritative edition. 258pp. 9⅜ × 12¼.   24187-4 Pa. **$11.95**

COMPLETE CONCERTI GROSSI IN FULL SCORE, Arcangelo Corelli. All 12 concerti in the famous late nineteenth-century edition prepared by violinist Joseph Joachim and musicologist Friedrich Chrysander. 240pp. 8⅜ × 11¼.   25606-5 Pa. **$11.95**

WATER MUSIC AND MUSIC FOR THE ROYAL FIREWORKS IN FULL SCORE, George Frideric Handel. Full scores of two of the most popular Baroque orchestral works performed today—reprinted from definitive Deutsche Handelgesellschaft edition. Total of 96pp. 8⅜ × 11.   25070-9 Pa. **$5.95**

LATER SYMPHONIES, Wolfgang A. Mozart. Full orchestral scores to last symphonies (Nos. 35–41) reproduced from definitive Breitkopf & Härtel Complete Works edition. Study score. 285pp. 9 × 12.   23052-X Pa. **$11.95**

17 DIVERTIMENTI FOR VARIOUS INSTRUMENTS, Wolfgang A. Mozart. Sparkling pieces of great vitality and brilliance from 1771-1779; consecutively numbered from 1 to 17. Reproduced from definitive Breitkopf & Härtel Complete Works edition. Study score. 241pp. 9⅜ × 12¼.   23862-8 Pa. **$11.95**

PIANO CONCERTOS NOS. 11–16 IN FULL SCORE, Wolfgang Amadeus Mozart. Authoritative Breitkopf & Härtel edition of six staples of the concerto repertoire, including Mozart's cadenzas for Nos. 12–16. 256pp. 9⅜ × 12¼.   25468-2 Pa. **$11.95**

PIANO CONCERTOS NOS. 17–22, Wolfgang Amadeus Mozart. Six complete piano concertos in full score, with Mozart's own cadenzas for Nos. 17–19. Breitkopf & Härtel edition. Study score. 370pp. 9⅜ × 12¼.   23599-8 Pa. **$14.95**

PIANO CONCERTOS NOS. 23–27, Wolfgang Amadeus Mozart. Mozart's last five piano concertos in full score, plus cadenzas for Nos. 23 and 27, and the Concert Rondo in D Major, K.382. Breitkopf & Härtel edition. Study score. 310pp. 9⅜ × 12¼.   23600-5 Pa. **$11.95**

CONCERTI FOR WIND INSTRUMENTS IN FULL SCORE, Wolfgang Amadeus Mozart. Exceptional volume contains ten pieces for orchestra and wind instruments and includes some of Mozart's finest, most popular music. 272pp. 9⅜ × 12¼.   25228-0 Pa. **$12.95**

THE VIOLIN CONCERTI AND THE SINFONIA CONCERTANTE, K.364, IN FULL SCORE, Wolfgang Amadeus Mozart. All five violin concerti and famed double concerto reproduced from authoritative Breitkopf & Härtel Complete Works Edition. 208pp. 9⅜ × 12½.   25169-1 Pa. **$10.95**

SYMPHONIES 88–92 IN FULL SCORE: The Haydn Society Edition, Joseph Haydn. Full score of symphonies Nos. 88 through 92. Large, readable noteheads, ample margins for fingerings, etc., and extensive Editor's Commentary. 304pp. 9 × 12. (Available in U.S. only)   24445-8 Pa. **$13.95**

COMPLETE LONDON SYMPHONIES IN FULL SCORE, Series I and Series II, Joseph Haydn. Reproduced from the Eulenburg editions are Symphonies Nos. 93–98 (Series I) and Nos. 99–104 (Series II). 800pp. 8⅜ × 11¼. (Available in U.S. only)   Series I 24982-4 Pa. **$14.95**
    Series II 24983-2 Pa. **$15.95**

FOUR SYMPHONIES IN FULL SCORE, Franz Schubert. Schubert's four most popular symphonies: No. 4 in C Minor ("Tragic"); No. 5 in B-flat Major; No. 8 in B Minor ("Unfinished"); and No. 9 in C Major ("Great"). Breitkopf & Härtel edition. Study score. 261pp. 9⅜ × 12¼.   23681-1 Pa. **$11.95**

GREAT OVERTURES IN FULL SCORE, Carl Maria von Weber. Overtures to *Oberon, Der Freischutz, Euryanthe* and *Preciosa* reprinted from authoritative Breitkopf & Härtel editions. 112pp. 9 × 12.   25225-6 Pa. **$6.95**

SYMPHONIES NOS. 1, 2, 3, AND 4 IN FULL SCORE, Ludwig van Beethoven. Republication of H. Litolff edition. 272pp. 9 × 12.   26033-X Pa. **$10.95**

SYMPHONIES NOS. 5, 6 AND 7 IN FULL SCORE, Ludwig van Beethoven. Republication of the H. Litolff edition. 272pp. 9 × 12.   26034-8 Pa. **$10.95**

SYMPHONIES NOS. 8 AND 9 IN FULL SCORE, Ludwig van Beethoven. Republication of the H. Litolff edition. 256pp. 9 × 12.   26035-6 Pa. **$10.95**

SIX GREAT OVERTURES IN FULL SCORE, Ludwig van Beethoven. Six staples of the orchestral repertoire from authoritative Breitkopf & Härtel edition. *Leonore Overtures,* Nos. 1–3; Overtures to *Coriolanus, Egmont, Fidelio.* 288pp. 9 × 12.   24789-9 Pa. **$12.95**

COMPLETE PIANO CONCERTOS IN FULL SCORE, Ludwig van Beethoven. Complete scores of five great Beethoven piano concertos, with all cadenzas as he wrote them, reproduced from authoritative Breitkopf & Härtel edition. New table of contents. 384pp. 9⅜ × 12¼.   24563-2 Pa. **$14.95**

GREAT ROMANTIC VIOLIN CONCERTI IN FULL SCORE, Ludwig van Beethoven, Felix Mendelssohn and Peter Ilyitch Tchaikovsky. The Beethoven Op. 61, Mendelssohn, Op. 64 and Tchaikovsky, Op. 35 concertos reprinted from the Breitkopf & Härtel editions. 224pp. 9 × 12.   24989-1 Pa. **$10.95**

MAJOR ORCHESTRAL WORKS IN FULL SCORE, Felix Mendelssohn. Generally considered to be Mendelssohn's finest orchestral works, here in one volume are: the complete *Midsummer Night's Dream; Hebrides Overture; Calm Sea and Prosperous Voyage Overture;* Symphony No. 3 in A ("Scottish"); and Symphony No. 4 in A ("Italian"). Breitkopf & Härtel edition. Study score. 406pp. 9 × 12.   23184-4 Pa. **$15.95**

COMPLETE SYMPHONIES, Johannes Brahms. Full orchestral scores. No. 1 in C Minor, Op. 68; No. 2 in D Major, Op. 73; No. 3 in F Major, Op. 90; and No. 4 in E Minor, Op. 98. Reproduced from definitive Vienna Gesellschaft der Musikfreunde edition. Study score. 344pp. 9 × 12.   23053-8 Pa. **$13.95**

Dover Chamber Music Scores

COMPLETE SUITES FOR UNACCOMPANIED CELLO AND SONATAS FOR VIOLA DA GAMBA, Johann Sebastian Bach. Bach-Gesellschaft edition of the six cello suites (BWV 1007–1012) and three sonatas (BWV 1027–1029), commonly played today on the cello. 112pp. 9⅜ × 12¼. 25641-3 Pa. **$7.95**

WORKS FOR VIOLIN, Johann Sebastian Bach. Complete Sonatas and Partitas for Unaccompanied Violin; Six Sonatas for Violin and Clavier. Bach-Gesellschaft edition. 158pp. 9⅜ × 12¼. 23683-8 Pa. **$7.95**

COMPLETE STRING QUARTETS, Wolfgang A. Mozart. Breitkopf & Härtel edition. All 23 string quartets plus alternate slow movement to K.156. Study score. 277pp. 9⅜ × 12¼. 22372-8 Pa. **$11.95**

COMPLETE STRING QUINTETS, Wolfgang Amadeus Mozart. All the standard-instrumentation string quintets, plus String Quintet in C Minor, K.406; Quintet with Horn or Second Cello, K.407; and Clarinet Quintet, K.581. Breitkopf & Härtel edition. Study score. 181pp. 9⅜ × 12¼. 23603-X Pa. **$8.95**

STRING QUARTETS, OPP. 20 and 33, COMPLETE, Joseph Haydn. Complete reproductions of the 12 masterful quartets (six each) of Opp. 20 and 33—in the reliable Eulenburg edition. 272pp. 8⅜ × 11¼. 24852-6 Pa. **$11.95**

STRING QUARTETS, OPP. 42, 50 and 54, Joseph Haydn. Complete reproductions of Op. 42 in D minor; Op. 50, Nos. 1–6 ("Prussian Quartets") and Op. 54, Nos. 1–3. Reliable Eulenburg edition. 224pp. 8⅜ × 11¼. 24262-5 Pa. **$9.95**

TWELVE STRING QUARTETS, Joseph Haydn. 12 often-performed works: Op. 55, Nos. 1–3 (including *Razor*); Op. 64, Nos. 1–6; Op. 71, Nos. 1–3. Definitive Eulenburg edition. 288pp. 8⅜ × 11¼. 23933-0 Pa. **$10.95**

ELEVEN LATE STRING QUARTETS, Joseph Haydn. Complete reproductions of Op. 74, Nos. 1–3; Op. 76, Nos. 1–6; and Op. 77, Nos. 1 and 2. Definitive Eulenburg edition. Full-size study score. 320pp. 8⅜ × 11¼. 23753-2 Pa. **$11.95**

COMPLETE STRING QUARTETS, Ludwig van Beethoven. Breitkopf & Härtel edition. Six quartets of Opus 18; three quartets of Opus 59; Opera 74, 95, 127, 130, 131, 132, 135 and Grosse Fuge. Study score. 434pp. 9⅜ × 12¼. 22361-2 Pa. **$15.95**

SIX GREAT PIANO TRIOS IN FULL SCORE, Ludwig van Beethoven. Definitive Breitkopf & Härtel edition of Beethoven's Piano Trios Nos. 1–6 including the "Ghost" and the "Archduke". 224pp. 9⅜ × 12¼. 25398-8 Pa. **$10.95**

COMPLETE VIOLIN SONATAS, Ludwig van Beethoven. All ten sonatas including the "Kreutzer" and "Spring" sonatas in the definitive Breitkopf & Härtel edition. 256pp. 9 × 12. 26277-4 Pa. **$12.95**

COMPLETE SONATAS AND VARIATIONS FOR CELLO AND PIANO, Ludwig van Beethoven. All five sonatas and three sets of variations. Reprinted from Breitkopf & Härtel edition. 176pp. 9⅜ × 12¼. 26441-6 Pa. **$9.95**

COMPLETE CHAMBER MUSIC FOR STRINGS, Franz Schubert. Reproduced from famous Breitkopf & Härtel edition: Quintet in C Major (1828), 15 quartets and two trios for violin(s), viola, and violincello. Study score. 348pp. 9 × 12. 21463-X Pa. **$13.95**

COMPLETE CHAMBER MUSIC FOR PIANOFORTE AND STRINGS, Franz Schubert. Breitkopf & Härtel edition. *Trout*, Quartet in F Major, and trios for piano, violin, cello. Study score. 192pp. 9 × 12. 21527-X Pa. **$9.95**

CHAMBER WORKS FOR PIANO AND STRINGS, Felix Mendelssohn. Eleven of the composer's best known works in the genre—duos, trios, quartets and a sextet—reprinted from authoritative Breitkopf & Härtel edition. 384pp. 9⅜ × 12¼. 26117-4 Pa. **$15.95**

COMPLETE CHAMBER MUSIC FOR STRINGS, Felix Mendelssohn. All of Mendelssohn's chamber music: Octet, Two Quintets, Six Quartets, and Four Pieces for String Quartet. (Nothing with piano is included.) Complete works edition (1874–7). Study score. 283pp. 9⅜ × 12¼. 23679-X Pa. **$12.95**

CHAMBER MUSIC OF ROBERT SCHUMANN, edited by Clara Schumann. Superb collection of three trios, four quartets, and piano quintet. Breitkopf & Härtel edition. 288pp. 9⅜ × 12¼. 24101-7 Pa. **$12.95**

COMPLETE SONATAS FOR SOLO INSTRUMENT AND PIANO, Johannes Brahms. All seven sonatas—three for violin, two for cello and two for clarinet (or viola)—reprinted from the authoritative Breitkopf & Härtel edition. 208pp. 9 × 12. 26091-7 Pa. **$10.95**

COMPLETE CHAMBER MUSIC FOR STRINGS AND CLARINET QUINTET, Johannes Brahms. Vienna Gesellschaft der Musikfreunde edition of all quartets, quintets, and sextet without piano. Study edition. 262pp. 8⅜ × 11¼. 21914-3 Pa. **$10.95**

QUINTET AND QUARTETS FOR PIANO AND STRINGS, Johannes Brahms. Full scores of *Quintet in F Minor*, Op. 34; *Quartet in G Minor*, Op. 25; *Quartet in A Major*, Op. 26; *Quartet in C Minor*, Op. 60. Breitkopf & Härtel edition. 298pp. 9 × 12. 24900-X Pa. **$13.95**

COMPLETE PIANO TRIOS, Johannes Brahms. All five piano trios in the definitive Breitkopf & Härtel edition. 288pp. 9 × 12. 25769-X Pa. **$12.95**

CHAMBER WORKS FOR PIANO AND STRINGS, Antonín Dvořák. Society editions of the F Minor and Dumky piano trios, D Major and E-flat Major piano quartets and A Major piano quintet. 352pp. 8⅜ × 11¼. (Available in U.S. only) 25663-4 Pa. **$13.95**

FIVE LATE STRING QUARTETS, Antonín Dvořák. Treasury of Czech master's finest chamber works: Nos. 10, 11, 12, 13, 14. Reliable Simrock editions. 282pp. 8½ × 11. 25135-7 Pa. **$11.95**

STRING QUARTETS BY DEBUSSY AND RAVEL/Claude Debussy: Quartet in G Minor, Op. 10/Maurice Ravel: Quartet in F Major, Claude Debussy and Maurice Ravel. Authoritative one-volume edition of two influential masterpieces noted for individuality, delicate and subtle beauties. 112pp. 8⅜ × 11. (Not available in France or Germany) 25231-0 Pa. **$6.95**

GREAT CHAMBER WORKS, César Franck. Four Great works: Violin Sonata in A Major, Piano Trio in F-sharp Minor, String Quartet in D Major and Piano Quintet in F Minor. From J. Hamelle, Paris and C. F. Peters, Leipzig editions. 248pp. 9⅜ × 12¼. 26546-3 Pa. **$13.95**

---

*Available from your music dealer or write for **free** Music Catalog to*
Dover Publications, Inc., Dept. MUBI, 31 East 2nd Street, Mineola, N.Y. 11501.